LEEDS

City Beautiful

LEEDS
City Beautiful

Nigel A. Ibbotson

breedon **books**
PUBLISHING

First published in Great Britain in 2009 by
The Breedon Books Publishing Company Limited
Breedon House, 3 The Parker Centre,
Derby, DE21 4SZ.

A catalogue record for this book is available from the
British Library.

ISBN 978-1-85983-678-1

Printed and bound by MKT Print, Slovenia

CONTENTS

PREFACE

I moved to Leeds in 1984 and lived there for the next 20 years. During this time I witnessed many changes: not only to many of the buildings but also to the attitudes of its inhabitants. I watched this city grow into a vibrant, exciting and positive place, which was prepared to embrace the 21st century with outstretched arms and with all the vigour it could muster. After leaving Leeds in 2004 I have, unfortunately, had little opportunity to visit. However, this project has meant that once more I was to frequent its streets. The changes in the last four years have been dramatic, to say the least. The city has seen the addition of many new buildings, some of which are already fast becoming landmarks in their own right. Through producing this book my respect and admiration for this great city has been rekindled.

Nigel A. Ibbotson
December 2008

ACKNOWLEDGEMENTS

I would like to thank the following people for their kind assistance, and without whose help this book would not have been possible: Rachel Moyise at the Grand Theatre, Amy Heydenrych of Aedas, Chris Tweedly at Leeds Central Library, Graham Dentith at Clarence Docks, Lloyd Ingram at Leeds Railway Station and John Martin, the press officer at Harewood House.

INTRODUCTION

Pro Rege et Lege

'For the King and the law'

Today the city of Leeds is one of the country's major metropolises; it is a vibrant place, with an exciting combination of outstanding old buildings and striking modern structures, which together guarantee that the city's rich legacy will continue far into the future.

Little is known of the origins of this historic place, but evidence has shown that it has been occupied by humans for at least 2,500 years. Artefacts dating from the Bronze Age have been unearthed throughout Leeds and the remains of an Iron Age earthwork discovered near to Rampart Road are thought to have been a fort.

Once, in prehistoric times, the region would have been covered with dense forests and swampy marshes, and slowly in the mists of time our forefathers began to clear away the trees, making the land inhabitable. We now know that they first settled in an area which was close to the present–day Leeds Bridge.

The origin of the city's name has been the subject of much debate and argument. One theory is that it was derived from the old Celtic name of *Ladenses*, meaning 'people by the fast flowing river'. The Venerable Bede, a Benedictine monk from Northumbria, wrote in his *Ecclesiastical History of the English People* in AD 731 of a place that he called 'Leodis'. Many believe that he was perhaps referring to Leeds. Perhaps we will never know for sure, but this does not lessen the impact of this stunning city.

As with many of its neighbours in West Yorkshire, Leeds was famous for its woollen and textile industries. At the beginning of the 19th century, however, engineers such as Matthew Murray, taking advantage of new innovations, were to establish Leeds as one of the world's most important centres for engineering. Indeed, it was not long before this industry took over from textiles as the biggest employers in the city.

Growth in the 19th century was phenomenal and Leeds soon became the fourth-largest town in England, earning the title of 'Capital of the North'. The century saw the population explode from a mere 50,000 to almost half a million people. Today, Leeds is the largest city in the whole of Yorkshire and can boast that it is one of the largest financial centres in England (outside the capital). In 2003 the city was voted Britain's Best City for Business by Omis Research (Europe's leading independent location consultants).

Each step through this delightful city reveals another facet of its exciting history; from the beautiful churches to stunningly ornate Victorian buildings such as Temple Mill, from ancient edifices to modern structures. A city that, although rightfully proud of its heritage, looks towards the future.

▶ *The iconic Leeds Town Hall, as viewed from the fountain in Millennium Square.*

LEEDS TOWN HALL

In 1852 a young architect from Hull called Cuthbert Brodrick won a competition held to find the design for Leeds Town Hall. It took six years to complete the construction, and the hall was opened by Queen Victoria. Leeds had become an important industrial centre, and the civic leaders of Leeds were keen to have a building which would reflect this; one which would stand as a symbol of confidence and civic pride. With Brodrick's iconic design, they were to have their wishes fulfilled.

*The tower is one of Leeds'
most recognisable landmarks.*

Initially, a few members of the council voiced their concerns because Brodrick had been unheard of prior to the competition and there were doubts about the safety of his design. The knighted architect Sir Charles Berry, who had been assessor for the competition, claimed that although he had never previously heard of Brodrick, he was confident that the design was safe. Sir Charles went on to further reassure the doubters by predicting that the 'new town hall would be the most perfect architectural gem outside London'; praise indeed from the architect of the Houses of Parliament.

▲ At each side of the main entrance is carved a cherub, draped with a sheepskin – no doubt a reference to the woollen industry, which was instrumental in the growth of Leeds.

▲ *The carving around the entrance of the town hall is the work of the prolific Victorian sculptor John Thomas (1813–1862).*

The site for the town hall had been purchased from a wealthy merchant and landowner named John Blayds for the sum of £9,500. A budget of £35,000 had been set for the build. Even at that time such a figure had been seen as inadequate to produce a building on such a grand scale, and a number of professional journals derided the paltry sum. It appears that many architects may have been in agreement for the competition only drew 16 entrants; far fewer than would normally be expected for such a prestigious project. The costs, however, were soon to rise and when the main contract was signed on 25 July 1853 the figure had already mounted to £41,835. The costs were to rise again with the addition of the tower, but by then the original figure had been totally forgotten.

Originally, the distinctive clock tower had not been part of Brodrick's design, but the civic leaders, keen to make an even grander statement, had insisted on one. This addition made the town hall the tallest building in Leeds – a record which it held until 1966.

At the grand entrance to this magnificent building lie four white lions, which are thought to have been inspired by the lions around Nelson's Column. These were the work of William Day Keyworth and were added to the town hall nine years after it was built. Legend has it that as the clock strikes midnight, the lions get up and walk around the building before resuming their positions. Sadly, time has not been too kind to these kingly beasts and their faces have almost been completely worn away by the weather. Even so, their regal bearing remains a pleasure for all to see.

THE WAR MEMORIAL

◀ *The War Memorial, with Leeds Town Hall in the background.*

The memorial was first unveiled on 14 October 1922 by Viscount Lascelles. It was designed by Sir Reginald Blomfield and had been sculpted by H.C. Fehr at a cost of £6,000 (which had been raised by public subscription). Originally, it was erected in City Square, but a new traffic scheme meant that it had to be moved to its present location in 1937. At the top of the monument is a bronze figure called the Angel of Peace, which was placed there in 1991 to replace the original Victory figure. The original figure was taken down for repairs in 1940, after a crack had been found in its base, and it was not restored until six years later. It was finally removed in 1965 when it moved during a gale. The head from the figure can now be found in the museum.

▼ *The Union Flags and the Angel of Peace on Remembrance Sunday.*

The Angel of Peace on top of the War Memorial.

▲ *A close-up of St George slaying the dragon.*

In October 1955 a flagstaff was erected behind the memorial. It had been the mainmast of the Isle of Man steamer *Viking*. The *Viking* had first seen action during World War One as a sea-plane carrier and again in 1939, when she was used to carry troops to France. She was also at the Dunkirk evacuation and later at the Normandy landings in 1944. The mast was rescued from a ship-breaker's yard.

▼ *The symbol of Leeds is an owl; there is one on each corner of the memorial.*

LEEDS CIVIC
HALL

▲ *The Civic Hall.*

If you travel down Cookridge Street you will come to the magnificent Leeds Civic Hall. This striking building was opened on 23 August 1933 by King George V. The building houses the council, which is composed of 99 councillors. It includes the Lord Mayor's office, council chambers and banqueting hall. Built during the Great Depression, it had been a job creation scheme of its day using unemployed workers to construct it, and it cost a total of £360,000. The building was designed by the English architect Emanuel Vincent Harris, who was chosen as the winner of a competition held in 1926 to design the hall.

▲ *The intricate wrought–iron gates that screen the main doors are by Wippell.*

▲ *The pediment, which contains the city's coat of arms and motto, is by John Hodge.*

The building is guarded by two magnificent gold owls standing on columns, the owl being the emblem of Leeds. Behind them are two equally exquisite gold clocks, and together in the bright sunlight they all make a truly wonderful sight.

*The gilded owls are
by John Hodge.*

▶ *The gilded clocks (one on each side of the building) were made in a late 17th century design.*

This impressive building overlooks Millennium Square, which was opened in December 2000 and is home to several large pieces of public art. Close to the civic hall stands a small marker obelisk, which is intended to draw one's attention to a plaque that commemorates the opening of Millennium Square by Nelson Mandela. The obelisk is made out of titanium (a modern material), which combined with its classic motif is thought to bring together ancient and modern.

▲ *The titanium obelisk outside the civic hall.*

MILLENNIUM SQUARE

▲ *The unique control tower (pictured here and on the previous page), called Off-Kilter, regulates the sound and lighting on the Millennium Square. It was created by Richard Wilson in 2000.*

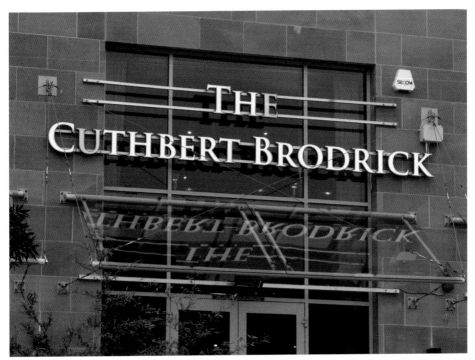

▲ *A bar on Millennium Square, named after the architect responsible for the Town Hall and the Corn Exchange.*

To mark the year 2000 celebrations, Leeds City Council, in partnership with the Millennium Commission, transformed the old Mandela Gardens and a rundown car park into one of Europe's most spectacular and innovative civic spaces – the Millennium Square. At a cost of £12 million, this flagship project gave the city its first new public square for over 60 years.

▲▶ *The fountain and water*
feature on Millennium Square.

The Millennium Square stands at the cultural heart of the city and is surrounded by some of Leeds' most famous and important buildings. It has become an exciting focal point, where various performances, such as outdoor theatre and music concerts (pop as well as classical), are performed. It also possesses a massive media screen, where news, local information and major events can be broadcast. Millennium Square is an ideal place to meet friends, relax and enjoy the entertainment.

▼ *Benches on Millennium Square.*

BOTH ARMS

This 1.6 metre high bronze sculpture was created by Leeds–born artist Kenneth Armitage. Entitled *Both Arms*, it is intended to represent a feeling of welcome to the city and is a monument to friendship.

LEEDS CITY MUSEUM

The Leeds Institute building, designed by Cuthbert Brodrick, has recently been redeveloped, and on 13 September 2008 it opened as the Leeds City Museum. Admission is free and as well as containing permanent displays, it also has a number of special exhibitions.

▲ *The decoration above the main entrance.*

Originally the City Museum was located on Park Row in a building that had been designed by Robert Dennis Chantrell in 1821. During World War Two it suffered extensive damage during an air raid. The building was repaired and continued to hold the museum until 1965, when it was relocated to Calverley Street, where it was housed with the Central Library.

In 1999 the museum closed and until it re-opened in 2008 Leeds had been without a permanent home for its collection.

▼ *The steps leading up to Leeds City Museum.*

LEEDS CENTRAL LIBRARY

Originally this building had been constructed to house the Municipal Offices. Prior to its grand opening on 17 April 1884, the various borough departments had been spread throughout the city. The building had been specifically designed to bring them all together. The architect responsible for this magnificent building was George Corson, who had beaten off 25 of his contemporaries in a competition to discover the winning design.

▶ *The magnificent stairwell was carved from limestone brought from Caen in Normandy. This limestone is softer than its English counterpart, which meant that it was easier for the stonemasons to carve. It does also mean, though, that it is more susceptible to damage.*

▲▲ The breathtaking Tiled Hall, originally the reading room, was converted to a sculpture gallery in 1888. In 1955 it became the Commercial and Technical Library, and in 1998 it changed to the Music Library. Today, it is the café. On the walls of the hall, terracotta portraits of the great writers can be found.

◀ The ceiling of the Tiled Hall is made up of hundreds of glazed hexagonal bricks by the Farnley Iron Company. Set among these are a number of gold bosses, which are part of an ingenious Victorian ventilation system.

▼ Detail of the tiles and a marble pillar.

▲▶ The remarkable animal carvings on the stairs were carved in Hopton Wood stone.

◀ The ceiling at the main entrance of the library.

▼ Another gilded owl; this time outside the Central Library.

◀ *The steps leading to Leeds Art Gallery.*

The original building was divided into a 'business side' and a 'popular side'. The business side took care of the borough's administration needs and was where the public came to pay their rates, gas and water bills; whereas the popular side was taken up with a free public library.

Over the years the building has seen a number of changes and once housed the

▲ *A bicycle stand outside the gallery.*

city's museum collection (this can now be found nearby in the old Leeds Institute building – see page 39). A programme of restoration was started in 1999 to return the building to its original splendour.

▼ *Next to the gallery is the Henry Moore Institute.*

Outside the gallery reclines the famous sculpture by Henry Moore.

▲ *The Victoria Hotel, designed by George Corson in 1865.*

▶▼ *In front of the institute is a plaque commemorating those servicemen from Leeds who were awarded the Victoria Cross.*

▲▼ *Considered by many to be one of Leeds' finest Victorian buildings is the School Board Offices, which were built in 1881. It was to open to mixed reviews, with some criticising the extravagance of the building, while others praised it, maintaining that it was 'one of the finest buildings in the country'.*

THE GENERAL INFIRMARY

In June 1767 a number of the town's gentlemen met at the New Inn to discuss the founding of 'an Infirmary for the Relief of the Sick and Hurt Poor within this Parish'. This initial meeting successfully raised a subscription of £352.10s.6d. The first infirmary was temporarily set up in the house of Mr Andrew Wilson on Kirkgate, but by the end of the year a new site was being sought for a purpose–built infirmary.

On 10 October 1768 the foundation stone was laid by Edwin Lascelles (Baron Harewood). The first infirmary was a red brick, two–storey building with stone–facing and was located on City Square, which at that time was almost in open country with unspoilt views to the river. Within three years of laying the foundation stone, the infirmary opened its doors and originally it had just 27 beds.

▼ *The General Infirmary, designed by Sir George Gilbert Scott, was constructed between 1863 and 1868.*

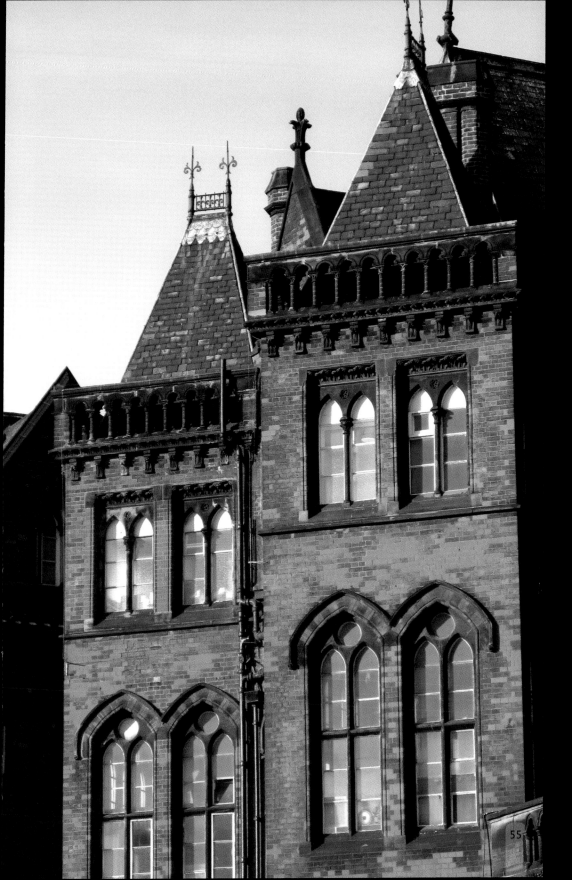

It soon became apparent that the new hospital was far too small for the rapidly growing population of Leeds, and by 1785 it became necessary to add a further storey and an extra wing. The infirmary now had 100 beds, and was described as 'one of the best hospitals in the kingdom'.

In 1861 the population of Leeds had reached almost a quarter of a million, which, combined with the influx of patients arriving from all over the West Riding, made it clear that the 150 beds that the infirmary then had were totally inadequate. Something had to be done, and fast, so it was decided that a new hospital was needed.

In 1864 the foundation stone was laid for the great Victorian hospital, on its new location of Great George Street (where it remains to this day). The new infirmary was designed by the renowned Victorian architect Sir George Gilbert Scott, and it incorporated all the latest thinking on sanitation and infection control. Much of this advice had been published by Miss Florence Nightingale.

The new building was officially opened in May 1868 by Prince Edward (later King Edward VII). The building was not immediately used for the purpose it was designed, and for a number of months the National Exhibition of Works of Art was stored there. In May 1869 a 10-year-old boy from Dewsbury became the first patient of the new infirmary. It was impractical to close the old infirmary immediately, and it was slowly emptied in phases. Eventually, the old building was demolished.

▲ *The Clarendon Wing, built in the 1960s.*

At a cost of £122,000, the new building provided around 300 beds, but even this number proved to be woefully inadequate and before long there were plans to add the first of many additions to the building. Over the years new wings were added to the hospital – for example, the Brotherton Wing was added in 1940 to cater for private patients. Shortly after it opened it was hit by a bomb by the Luftwaffe, fortunately emerging more or less unscathed. In the 1960s the Clarendon Wing was added.

Today the infirmary is a far cry from those early days when it had only 27 beds, being now the largest teaching hospital in Europe with buildings spreading over eight sites. It employs over 14,000 staff and treats around one million patients a year. It also now has a few more beds – 1,103 to be precise.

▼*Carpe Diem.*

HEPPER & SONS

The façade of the Victorian auctioneers and surveyors Hepper & Sons, which can be found on East Parade, is unmistakeably Italian Gothic in style. The walls and window sills of an earlier 18th–century house are still preserved in the basement. This Grade II listed building was rebuilt for the auctioneers in 1863 by George Corson. In 1911 the ground floor windows were enlarged by William Bakewell, when his Pearl Assurance Buildings were built opposite.

▲►▼*The front entrance to Hepper & Sons, auctioneers.*

61

A building on Park Row.

▲*East Parade Chambers was built in 1899 as offices for accountants, lawyers and assurance companies.*

▶ *At the corner of East Parade and the Headrow stand the Pearl Assurance Buildings (pictured here and overleaf), built in 1911 by William Bakewell.*

◀*Further along East Parade was the offices of the County Fire and Provident Life Association, built in 1870. Standing on the roof is a statue of Britannia accompanied by a lion.*

CITY SQUARE

▼▶The Black Prince *by Thomas Brock on City Square (also pictured on the previous page). This magnificent statue was made in Belgium and took seven years to complete. It was brought to Leeds via Hull and along the Aire & Calder Navigation.*

The City Square was created in 1897 to improve the open space in front of the old Post Office. It was to become the location of a number of Leeds' fine collection of statues, perhaps the most famous being that of the Black Prince. This was a gift from Colonel

Thomas Walter Harding, who had been Lord Mayor of Leeds between 1898 and 1899. Although the Prince had no connection with the City of Leeds, Harding felt that the son of Edward III symbolised the virtues of democracy and chivalry. Near to the Prince stand eight light standards in the shape of nymphs, by the architectural sculptor Alfred Drury (1859-1944).

Also standing in City Square are the statues of James Watt, Dr Hook (Vicar of Leeds), Joseph Priestley and the 16th-century benefactor of Leeds, John Harrison.

▲ *A lion from the base of* The Black Prince.

▼ *In the square are eight nymphs holding lamps; they are by Alfred Drury and called* Morn *and* Even.

The statues outside the Post Office of (left to right) James Watt, John Harrison, Dr Hook and Joseph Priestly.

JOHN HARRISON

John Harrison spent his entire life concerned with the welfare of Leeds and its inhabitants. His father was a wealthy cloth merchant and had bequeathed his son a substantial sum, and with his inheritance John was able to buy a considerable amount of land. In 1624 he built a new Grammar School on his own estate.

John was also instrumental in obtaining a Royal Charter from the king. After the Charter was granted he became the alderman's deputy and was later to become alderman in his own right. In 1629 he joined with a number of others to purchase the manor of Leeds and bring it under the control of the

corporation. Renowned for his acts of generosity and his tireless work for the poor and needy, perhaps his best known act of benefaction was the building of St John's Church. The church was built entirely at his own expense during the years 1631-34.

It is known that during the English Civil War he had Royalist sympathies and there is an interesting story about an incident that took place in 1647 while Charles I was imprisoned in Leeds. It is said John brought him a tankard, which was thought to contain ale but was in fact filled with gold sovereigns – possibly to bribe his jailors.

◄►*John Harrison by H.C. Fehr (who also sculpted the War Memorial).*

DR HOOK

Although not a locally born man, Dr Hook was to make Leeds his home and played a major part in the religious affairs of this great city during the 19th century. Born in London on 13 March 1798, Walter Farquhar Hook took Holy Orders after obtaining a degree at Christ Church, Oxford. He became vicar of Leeds in 1837 and, although it was not a unanimous decision to employ him, he soon won over his detractors.

▲▼ *Dr Hook by F.W. Pomeroy.*

His first meeting with his churchwardens, however, proved not to be the most auspicious, when he discovered that a number of them had put their hats and coats on the altar. To make matters worse, some were even sitting on it. He told them that this would be the last time and from then on he locked the church.

Many of his ideas proved unpopular with local people, but he worked tirelessly to help the poor, the sick and those less able to help themselves. He was a workaholic who began his day at 5.30am with three to four hours of serious writing. When Leeds Town Hall was opened by Queen Victoria in 1858, he was asked to lead the procession. In 1859 he was offered the Deanery of Chichester,

▲Statues on City Square. James Watt (left) next to John Harrison (right).

and before he left a banquet was arranged. He was presented with a casket, which had a view of the parish church on the front. Inside the casket were 2,000 guineas. But it was the gift of a pair of boots from a poor shoemaker that delighted him the most. During his tenure in Leeds he was responsible for the construction of 21 churches, around 30 schools and 23 parsonages. In 1903 his statue was erected in City Square, where it stands today to remind us of this remarkable man.

▲▶ Detail of the ornate façade of the General Post Office, which was built in 1896 by Sir Henry Tanner. It was constructed on the site of the Mixed Cloth Hall. The building is no longer used as a post office and now houses a number of bars and restaurants.

◀ *Number One, City Square; a thoroughly postmodern building by Abbey Hanson Rowe, built between 1996–98.*

▼ *By the main entrance is the sculpture of a flock of seagulls ascending towards the sky.*

LEEDS CASTLE

LEEDS MANOR HOUSE
The medieval manor house stood here on 'Castle Hill'. Its deep moat looped between the river and Boar Lane. Richard Wilson lavishly rebuilt it in 1765 and in 1823 it became Henry Scarbrough's hotel. The present-day pub is a surviving extension.

Many centuries ago Leeds lay in the shadow of a castle. Today no trace of this stronghold remains, which means we have to rely on other clues to suggest that it ever existed. Fortunately, there are a number of these to support Leeds' claim to once possessing a castle. We know roughly where its keep would have stood because a blue plaque attached to the present-day Scarbrough Hotel refers to a mediaeval manor house which once stood there surrounded by a moat.

Further evidence that a castle once stood in this place can be found in the name, for it was called 'Castle Hill'. It is said that King Stephen laid

The mirrored façade of the Bourse reflects the building opposite.

siege to the castle at Leeds when travelling north to fight the Scots. In 1765 the manor house (the castle had long gone by this time) was rebuilt by Richard Wilson and in 1823 it became Henry Scarbrough's hotel. The present-day building which stands near Leeds railway station is a surviving extension of this hotel.

LEEDS RAILWAY STATION

The railways first came to Leeds in 1834, when the North Eastern Railway opened its line between Leeds and Selby. This first line terminated to the east of the city at Marsh Lane. Six years later the North Midland Railway built a line from Derby to Leeds, which terminated to the south of the city. It was extended to Wellington Street in 1846 to create a more centrally located terminus. This became known as Wellington Station. In 1854 Central Station was opened and 15 years later a further station was opened called New Station.

For the next 67 years these stations remained separate, until 1938 when New Station and Wellington Station were combined to form Leeds City Station. It was around this time that the Queen's Hotel was built. Central Station was to remain separate.

In 1967 all trains were diverted into the City Station, and Central Station was closed and later demolished. Leeds now had only one central station to serve the city. Recently £245 million has been spent modernising it station and bringing it into the 21st century. The new improvements allow for increased traffic and faster trains.

▲◀ The elaborately ornate Yorkshire Penny Bank was designed by G.B. Bulmer in 1893 in the Baronial Gothic style, complete with gargoyles and spires.

▲ An excellently carved dog's head.

▲▶ *A wrought-iron gate and some intricate carving.*

THE QUEEN'S HOTEL

Another of Leeds' iconic buildings is Queen's Hotel, with is elegant Art Deco designs. This handsome building dominates the south side of City Square. It was designed by W.H. Hamlyn, architect for London Midland & Scottish Railway. The interior of this magnificent hotel was designed by W. Curtis Green, who was responsible for fitting out London's famous Dorchester Hotel in the 1930s. The Queen's Hotel was built in 1937 and the 10-storey building was faced with Portland stone. It has 232 rooms in total, 33 of which are suites. In 2003 this four-star hotel was given a £10 million face-lift. The hotel prides itself on offering a first-class service.

ATLAS HOUSE

At the junction of King Street and St Paul's Street stands the imposing Atlas House, which was built in 1910 by Perkin & Bulmer in Renaissance style. This five-storey block of insurance offices was constructed in concrete using the Kahn system, a system for reinforcing concrete that was developed by the American industrial architect Albert Kahn (1869-1942). A remarkable feature of this building is the ornate sculpture of Atlas struggling under the weight of the world on his shoulders. This delightful figure was created by Thewlis & Co.

▲▼ *King Street.*

HOTEL METROPOLE

Without doubt one of the most distinctive hotels in Leeds, with its ornate red terracotta façade, is the Hotel Metropole. Located on King Street, it was designed by the Leeds–based architectural practice of Chorley & Connon in 1897.

▼ *The stone cupola, which was retained from the White Cloth Hall.*

Built on the site of the White Cloth Hall, the hotel was opened in 1899. An interesting feature of the hotel is the stone cupola which was retained from the White Cloth Hall.

Recently this Grade II listed hotel has undergone a £6 million refurbishment, to give the interior a modern feeling while retaining its historic appearance.

PARK SQUARE

Built on the site of the mediaeval park of the Manor of Leeds, this fashionable and elegant square was created as a high–class residential area. In 1628 Charles I sold off the manor and the park was split into small plots. The site of the manor house and a number of the plots were inherited by the Wilson family at the end of the 17th century. In 1767 a building lease was granted by Richard Wilson, which allowed the development of residential properties on a site that covered 140 acres.

▼ *A row of properties on Park Square; the Town Hall can be seen in the background.*

ARRIDET   ARIDUM

▲ *This was the headquarters of the Bedford Level Corporation, who were responsible for fenland drainage. The motto ARRIDET ARIDUM means 'Dryness Pleaseth'.*

Building work began on Park Square in 1788. In the centre of the square was a good sized garden, which is still there today. Due to the outbreak of war with France, the development was never fully completed. The war meant that people had less money to invest in property, and by 1792 the Wilson family had become absentee landlords and simply lost interest in the development. The following year Benjamin Gott built his new mill on land nearby and smoke from this and other mills in the vicinity became a nuisance to the high-class residents. The final straw came when cheap back-to-backs were built between Gott's mill and Park Square. Fearing infectious diseases, those residents who could afford to do so moved to more salubrious areas further out of town.

▶ *Overleaf: Park Square Gardens, with Sir John Barran's Victorian warehouse in the background.*

▲◄ *Flowers in Park Square Gardens.*

◄►▼ *Many of the buildings on Park Square show off delightful terracotta façades.*

▲*Steps leading to a basement in park square.*

▲ *One of the properties displays a window box.*

At the beginning of the 19th century the area became the business quarter of the town and the elegant homes on Park Square were converted into offices. Due to its close vicinity to the courts, the square now houses the offices of a number of solicitors and legal practices. Although the residents have long since left, without the pollution from the mills' billowing chimneys the elegance of the square has returned.

▲▼◄The Oxford Place Methodist Church. James Simpson originally built the chapel in 1835, but between 1896 and 1903 work was carried out to remodel the building to face the town hall. This project was carried out by G.F. Danby and W.H. Thorp. The building was constructed from local red brick and dressed with strips of stone from nearby Morley Moor.

▲▶▼*Built in the Moorish style is the elegant Gresham House, which can be found on St Paul's Street.*

GRESHAM HOUSE

7

THE BOULES PLAYER

In Bond Court a Yorkshire family stand watching a Frenchman playing boules – the group is a bronze sculpture created by Roger Burnett in 2000. Next to the sculpture is a patch of grey gravel, which is an actual boules court. For those wishing to while away some time, there are boules and instructions available.

THE GRAND THEATRE

Leeds Grand Theatre and Opera House first opened its doors on 18 November 1878. The first performance to grace the boards in this magnificent theatre was Shakespeare's *Much Ado About Nothing*. The building had been designed by the architect George Corson, who had been greatly influenced during this project by his assistant James Robertson Watson.

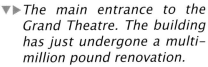

▼▶The main entrance to the Grand Theatre. The building has just undergone a multi-million pound renovation.

Watson had undertaken a tour of Europe's churches and theatres, and his experiences were reflected in the final design of the Grand. The construction took 13 months to complete and cost a total of £62,000.

When it first opened the auditorium possessed an interesting safety feature: as it was lit by gas there was a constant danger of fire and in the event of such an emergency the light fittings converted to water–sprinklers at a moment's notice.

Audiences have been entertained in this splendid theatre for well over 100 years. Recent redevelopment and restoration of this magnificent building has guaranteed its future and there can be no doubt that audiences will be entertained in these lavish surroundings for many years to come.

▶ *Another entrance to the theatre.*

▶ *Overleaf: The auditorium as seen from one of the boxes.*

117

▲ *The stunning detailing is made of papier–mâché.*

◄ *The auditorium from the stage.*

On the first floor one is greeted by the great bard in a contemplative mood.

LEEDS CATHEDRAL

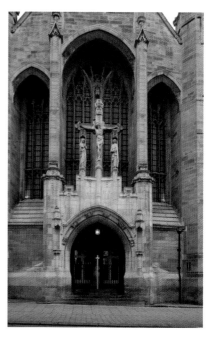

Although the Church of St Anne did not open its doors until October 1838, its history began in 1786. It was in that year that Father Albert Underhill, a Dominican priest, obtained some rooms off Briggate for the purpose of worship. It was to be the first Catholic place of worship in Leeds since the Reformation. These rooms served the small Catholic community in the town for eight years until 1794, when a purpose–built chapel was opened on Lady Lane called St Mary's. By the 1830s the Catholic population of Leeds was growing rapidly. This was mainly due to an influx of Irish settlers. To cater for this growth a new chapel was opened on York Road in 1831 called St Patrick's. Five years later a site in the centre of Leeds was obtained for a new church. Designed by John Child, a local architect, the new church opened its doors in October 1838 and was dedicated to St Anne; this was in honour of Anne Humble, who was the late sister of two of the church's principal benefactors, Sarah and Grace Humble.

In 1878 the church was given cathedral status, but 20 years later the church was compulsorily purchased by Leeds Corporation and demolished. A replacement site was needed and after considering a number of alternatives the congregation decided that they should accept the corporation's offer of land. Work on the present cathedral started in 1901 and took only three years to complete. It was designed by a London–based architect, John Henry Eastwood (1843–1913).

Aided by his assistant, Sydney Kyffin Greenslade (1866–1955), they produced an impressive design in the Arts and Crafts neo–Gothic style. The cathedral was still not finished when the first service was held on 1 May 1904.

Enshrined in the altar are two skulls dating from the 16th century and they are thought to have belonged to Father Peter Snow and his companion Ralph Grimston. Both had been martyred in York on 15 June 1598 for their refusal to conform to the Church of England. Father Peter Snow had originated from Ripon, where his father, Matthew Snow, had been the wakeman in 1545. His companion, Ralph Grimston, was a gentleman from Nidd. After they had been executed their severed heads were impaled on spikes and left as a grim warning to others.

▼ *A shop window opposite the cathedral.*

▲ *An interesting wrought–iron dome.*

▲ *The Leeds College of Art and Design – this large mosaic panel was designed by the professor of painting and mural design Gerald Moira. It was made by Rust & Co in their 'new vitreous mosaic'. The two figures represent the muses 'Art' and 'Design'.*

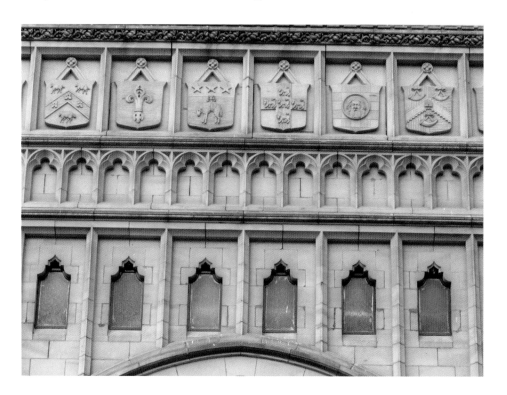

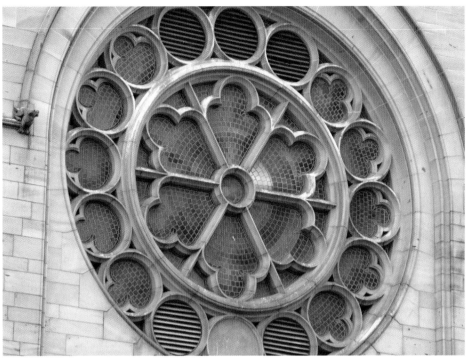

▲▶◀ *The Coliseum Theatre –*
built by William Bakewell
in 1895. It was converted
from a concert hall, which
had been opened 10
years earlier by the Prince
and Princess of Wales. In
the early 20th century
it became a cinema,
in which capacity it
remained until 1961,
when it was closed. Since
then it has been used as
a film and TV studio,
bingo hall, a music venue
and a nightclub. It has
recently undergone a
renovation and the Grade
I listed building is now
the venue for the Leeds
Academy (run by The
Academy Music Group).

CHURCHES IN LEEDS

There are no mediaeval churches left in the centre of Leeds, instead you have to travel to the outskirts, where you can find, for example, a delightful Norman church in the suburb of Adel. There are, however, a number of churches in the city centre which are of interest; the oldest being St John's on New Briggate, which was built between 1631 and 1634. Its construction was paid for by the Leeds benefactor John Harrison. An interesting feature is that this church has two naves. It should also be noted that there are few large churches in England dating from that period.

▶ *St John's Church with its sundial over the door.*

▼ *Detail of the gate to the church porch.*

SO TEACH US TO NUMBER OUR
DAYS THAT WE MAY APPLY OUR
HEARTS UNTO WISDOM

▶▼◀The Neoclassical steeple of Holy Trinity was added over 100 years after Halfpenny built this church in 1727.

Another remarkable church is Holy Trinity on Boar Lane. This graceful church was first opened in 1727 and its design by William Halfpenny is unmistakeably of the Georgian period. The west tower was added in 1839 and was the work of Robert Dennis Chantrell, a church architect. He is perhaps best known for designing Leeds Parish Church.

LEEDS PARISH CHURCH

There has been a church at this site since at least the early seventh century. This church was destroyed by fire in AD 633, and the church that stands here today was built in the 19th century. Its construction had been commissioned by Dr Walter Farquhar Hook and it cost £26,000 to build. The architect was Robert Dennis Chantrell. The church was dedicated to St Peter and consecrated on 2 September 1841; among the congregation was Florence Nightingale. It possesses one of the finest organs to be found in any English parish church.

▼*East Bar - this stone marks what once was the eastern boundary of mediaeval Leeds. The stone has been built into the wall that surrounds the parish church.*

▼*The ultra-modern Bridgewater Place can be seen in the distance.*

▶*Frozen leaves and the parish church in the background.*

*The Parish
Church of St
Peter's.*

LEEDS BRIDGE

The bridge that we see today was built in 1871 and much of the stone used in its construction was removed from Kirkstall Abbey. The metalwork of the bridge includes a large, detailed city crest. It is not known when the first bridge was built here, but we do know for certain that there has been one since the 14th century. Evidence suggests, however, that there would have been some form of crossing here since at least Saxon times.

In 1888 the bridge was the site of one of the first-ever movies made by Louis Aimé Augustin Le Prince, a French inventor. Previously he had filmed his wife at one of the city's parks (Roundhay) and the bridge would be the site of his second experiment. Sadly, he died two years later under mysterious circumstances and never received the recognition that he deserved as the 'Father of Cinema'.

BRIGGATE

One of the main thoroughfares of the city is Briggate and in Old English the name means 'Road to the Bridge'. When the lord of the manor was granted permission to create a new town in 1207, he built it on a street running north from a crossing on the River Aire. The charter gave him permission to divide the land into 60 building plots which he rented out for the sum of 16 pennies per plot per year. Briggate was wide enough to hold markets and fairs and even today a number of events are held along this ancient road. It is still at the heart of Leeds, being the location of a number of well-known departmental stores and shops.

▼ *The ancient thoroughfare.*

▲ *The Time Ball Buildings. Behind the stucco decorated façade, which was applied by John Dyson in 1876, stand two 17th-century houses.*

There are a number of arcades which lead off from Briggate. The first of these to be constructed was the Gothic designed Thornton's Arcade, which was built in 1878 by Charles Thornton. The arcade has a pointed glass vault, which complements its Gothic theme. Other interesting features include a sculptured head of a young woman (which was based on a painting by Gainsborough) and a fabulous clock, complete with figures based on characters from Sir Walter Scott's *Ivanhoe*.

▶ *The building got its name from an intricate ball mechanism, which was linked to Greenwich, and at 1.00pm each day the ball would drop. This was installed in 1910.*

▲Dyson was a watchmaker and jeweller. The building is now a restaurant.

▲ A second clock was also installed in 1910, upon which stood a gilded figure of Father Time, made by J.W. Appleyard.

▲▶ The Yorkshire Building Society: this building was constructed in pale cream terracotta. The fine detailing is unmistakeably baroque in style.

◀ *The Marks & Spencer building on Briggate is the only example of its type outside of London. Built by Norman Jones & Rigby of Southport, it was constructed to the modular design conceived by Marks & Spencer's consultant architect Robert Lutyens. Work on this building began in 1939 but was not completed until after World War Two had finished.*

Marks & Spencer was founded in 1893 in Leeds, when Michael Marks, a Polish refugee, formed a partnership with Tom Spencer. Michael had originally opened a stall in Kirkgate Market in 1884 and Tom had been a cashier for I.J. Dewhirst, the wholesale company which had supplied Michael Marks.

▼ *In complete contrast to its rather austere neighbour (the M&S building) are the former premises of Thornton & Co., India Rubber Manufacturers.*

▲ *A building detail on Briggate.*

Directly opposite Thornton's arcade can be found County Arcade, which together with Cross Arcade make up the luxurious Victoria Quarter. This area was lavishly designed by Frank Matcham, the theatre architect, and was built around 1900. Extensive use of marble and mosaics combined with upmarket shops make this a truly elegant shopping experience.

City Varieties has changed very little since it first opened in 1865, when it was built as an extension of the music room of the White Swan Inn. It is perhaps best known for being the home of the BBC's longest running variety show The Good Old Days, *which ran from 1953 to 1983.*

▶ *Outside the theatre are a number of characters from screen and stage.*

▲ Thornton's Arcade.

▼ The famous clock in Thornton's Arcade with its characters from Ivanhoe.

▶ Detail of the arcade's glass vaulted roof.

▲ The entrance to the Cross Arcade.

▼ Stonework above the entrance to the County Arcade.

▶ Detail from inside County Arcade, which was designed by Frank Matcham.

153

▲▼ *The circular mosaics on the floor of the arcade are by J. Veevers.*

155

◀▲*Shops along Queen's Arcade.*

▲▼ *The Victoria Quarter, home to many luxurious shops.*

▲▶ *The Grand Arcade, built in the Renaissance style.*

CORN EXCHANGE

Cuthbert Brodrick's iconic Corn Exchange.

The Corn Exchange building is considered by some to be one of the finest examples of Victorian architecture still standing in Britain today. The Corn Exchange was designed by a young architect from Hull called Cuthbert Brodrick. He had already gained international recognition for his work on Leeds Town Hall. The Corn Exchange was opened in 1864 and had been built for merchants to trade in corn and cereals, although it is now no longer used for this purpose and today it houses a variety of trendy shops.

▶ *A detail of the Corn Exchange's diamond-pointed rusticated stone, which was sourced locally.*

SIR JOHN BARRAN

▲ *The elegant minarets adorning the top of Sir John Barran's warehouse.*

The 19th-century industrialist Sir John Barran was a pioneer in the manufacture of ready-to-wear clothing. Soon after moving to Leeds in 1842, he opened a tailoring shop at 30 Bridge End South. It was not long, however, before he had moved to Briggate. His business prospered and in 1851 he opened a factory which had around 30 sewing machines. But it was while watching a band-saw cutting wood veneers that he thought of a major development, which would revolutionise the ready-to-wear industry. By the 1870s his factory would have 2,000 machines.

In 1878 Barran had a warehouse built in Park Square. This fabulous building was designed in the Moorish style by Thomas Ambler. The fine detailing on this building is simply stunning. This show-piece building is made of brick and terracotta, with delightful blue inlays around a giant segment-headed arch. The building is truly a masterpiece. The warehouse is known as St Paul's House and today houses a variety of offices.

As well as his business interests, Sir John was a Justice of the Peace, Mayor of Leeds from 1870 to 1871 and a Member of Parliament. In 1871 he acquired the estate of Roundhay, which he presented to the people of Leeds. He died in 1905 at the age of 83.

ARTHUR LOUIS AARON VC

At the bottom of Eastgate stands a statue which pays tribute to a brave young man. Arthur Louis Aaron was only 21 years old when he performed his selfless deed, which won him his Victoria Cross but cost him his life. On 12 August 1943 Flight Sergeant Aaron and his crew were flying a Short Stirling heavy bomber on a raid over Turin, Italy. The aircraft was badly damaged by gunfire, which put the front and rear gun turrets out of action, shatted the windscreen, damaged the elevator controls and three of the aeroplane's engines.

But much worse was the damage inside. The navigator had been killed outright and other crew members had been wounded. Arthur had also received terrible injuries from the gunfire. His jaw was shattered and part of his face had been torn away. He had also been wounded in his lung and his right arm was useless. Slumping forward over his controls, the aircraft fell into a nosedive, but after falling thousands of feet the flight engineer managed to regain control of the damaged aeroplane at 3,000ft. Due to Arthur's dreadful injuries he was unable to speak, but he gestured to the bomb aimer, urging him to take over the controls.

With one engine out of action, a course was set southwards to fly the stricken plane either to Sicily or North Africa. Arthur was taken to the rear of the aeroplane, where he was given morphine to dull the pain. Still determined to fulfil his responsibilities as captain of the crippled Stirling, he insisted on returning to the cockpit. With the help of other members of the crew he was lifted into his seat and they placed his feet onto the rudder bar. After making two attempts to take control, it became obvious that as he was weakened by his injuries he no longer had the strength to hold the unstable craft.

Unable to fly the plane and in great pain despite the morphine, he wrote instructions with his left hand. The flight home had taken five hours and by the time the flare path at Bone airfield was spotted, fuel was dangerously low. Summoning his failing strength, Arthur directed the bomb aimer to begin the hazardous job of bringing the crippled plane in to land.

▲ *The memorial to Arthur Louis Aaron VC.*

170

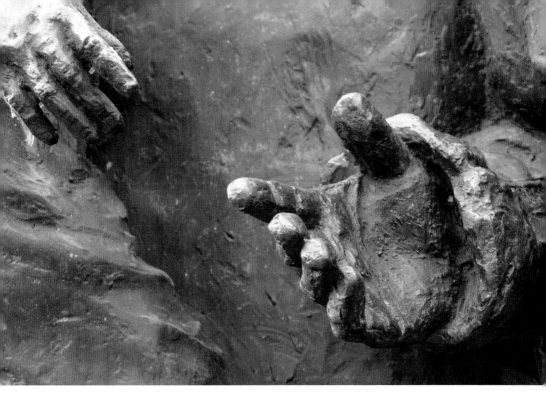

In darkness and with no undercarriage this would be a difficult task, and it was not until the fifth attempt that the Stirling was safely on the ground. By this time the exertion had been so great that Arthur was near to collapsing and had to be held by the crew.

Sadly, Arthur died nine hours after landing through exhaustion. If he had lain still and conserved his energy, he would have in all probability survived his wounds. He saw it as his duty to bring his crew and aircraft home safely and for neither of them to fall into enemy hands. A very brave young man indeed.

Today, his Victoria Cross is displayed in Leeds City Museum. On 24 March 2001 the bronze statue of this remarkable young hero was fittingly unveiled by the last survivor from the aircraft, Malcolm Mitchem. The sculpture was created by artist Graham Ibbeson and portrays Arthur Aaron standing next to a tree, in which three children are climbing. The children represent the passage of time between 1950 and 2000. The girl at the top is releasing a dove of peace and the three children represent the freedom that Arthur's ultimate sacrifice helped to secure.

The girl at the top of the memorial
is releasing a dove of peace.

QUARRY HILL

Over the centuries Leeds has been ravaged by the plague on a number of occasions. In 1645 the bubonic plague struck in the vicinity of Vicar Lane and that year 1,300 souls succumbed to the deadly disease. In the 17th century a number of 'plague' cabins were constructed outside what was then the city boundary at Quarry Hill. Once a person was suspected of having the plague they were quickly deposited in one of the cabins before they could infect anyone else.

During the 18th century the area became fashionable for the taking of the waters, when it was discovered that the water contained high quantities of

▼*A view towards Quarry Hill.*

▶ *The West Yorkshire Playhouse first opened its doors in March 1990. Since opening, the theatre has earned well-deserved international acclaim.*

sulphur. In the 1780s extensive building took place in Quarry Hill and it is thought to be one of the oldest inhabited areas of the city. It is possible that the area had been inhabited many centuries earlier as earthworks indicate the possibility of an early fort. By the 1830s Quarry Hill was overcrowded and the unsanitary conditions with which the population lived led to frequent epidemics of diseases such as typhoid and cholera. In 1910 these unhealthy conditions eventually resulted in a proposal to demolish the slums and start a programme of rebuilding.

Eventually the area was cleared and the Quarry Hill flats were built. These flats were built by Leeds City Council and modelled on Karl Marx Hof flats in Vienna. At that time the Quarry Hill flats were the largest housing scheme in the country and featured many of the latest ideas.

▶ *The Playhouse is the largest regional repertory theatre in the United Kingdom outside of London and Stratford.*

▲ *The Leeds College of Music. The LCM was first founded in 1965 and quickly developed a reputation as a leader in jazz education. It was not until 1997 that the college moved into these purpose-built premises.*

The first occupants moved into the flats in 1938, but work was to continue on them for some time after. In 1978 the whole complex was demolished as the concrete-clad steel frame construction had proved disastrous.

More recently, major redevelopment of the area has seen the additions of the West Yorkshire Playhouse, Leeds College of Music and the offices of the DWP (some refer to this dramatic building as 'Gotham City'; perhaps a reference to the strange structure on top of the building). Today Quarry Hill is the cultural quarter of Leeds.

▶ *The BBC in Leeds.*

177

▲ *The morning sun lights up West Riding House.*

▼ *The clock at Leeds City Bus Station.*

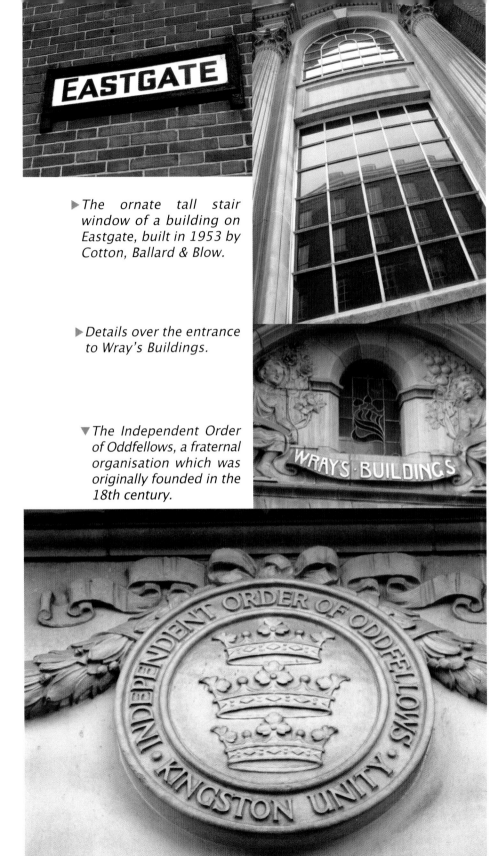

▶The ornate tall stair window of a building on Eastgate, built in 1953 by Cotton, Ballard & Blow.

▶Details over the entrance to Wray's Buildings.

▼The Independent Order of Oddfellows, a fraternal organisation which was originally founded in the 18th century.

THE MARKET

▶A brass dragon in the pavement outside Leeds City Market.

After the Central Market (located next to the Corn Exchange) burnt down in 1983, it was decided that it would be the ideal opportunity to build a new market which would better cater for modern needs. The council decided they wanted a building that would rival those of cities such as Bradford and Huddersfield. A competition was held to decide the design and by some coincidence the architects who won were John and Joseph Leeming of London, who had designed Halifax Town Hall (a design which the council had greatly admired).

It was originally estimated that it would cost £73,000 to construct; however, when the final building was opened in July 1904, the total cost had increased to £116,750. The market was officially opened by G.W. Balfour, who was the president of the board of trade and MP for Central Leeds.

▼A dragon inside the market.

▲ *A cherub at one of the entrances to the market.*

▲ Art in Leeds.

▲Many of the buildings in Leeds have exquisite architectural details, which are a pleasure to see.

◄ *This building has the city crest and motto over its entrance.*

▼ *A copper-domed building on the corner of Boar Lane.*

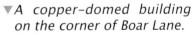

A MODERN OUTLOOK

As well as its rich heritage, Leeds is looking towards the future and has embraced the 21st century with open arms. Currently the city is undergoing massive re-development and there are certainly exciting times ahead. With its location on a direct link to London, by motorway, rail or plane, the commuter can be in the capital within a relatively short time.

▼ *A modern building which resembles a painting by Piet Mondrian.*

▲*Bridgewater Place, the tallest building in Yorkshire.*

Recent development has resulted in Bridgewater Place. This outstanding building has 32 floors, making it the tallest in Yorkshire. It was designed by Aedas Architects, who have been responsible for many innovative buildings throughout the world. Plans for this office and residential development were first announced in 2000; however, a number of delays prevented work commencing until 2004. It was completed in 2007. This magnificent building can be seen from up to 25 miles away.

Another development that has recently opened is Clarence Dock, which is destined to be the hottest new shopping experience in Leeds.

▼ *Clarence Dock. Opened by the television presenter and fashion consultant Gok Wan in 2008, this ultra–modern development includes apartments, offices, a hotel, casinos and luxury shops.*

▼▶Some of the fabulous new buildings that can be found at the Clarence Dock development.

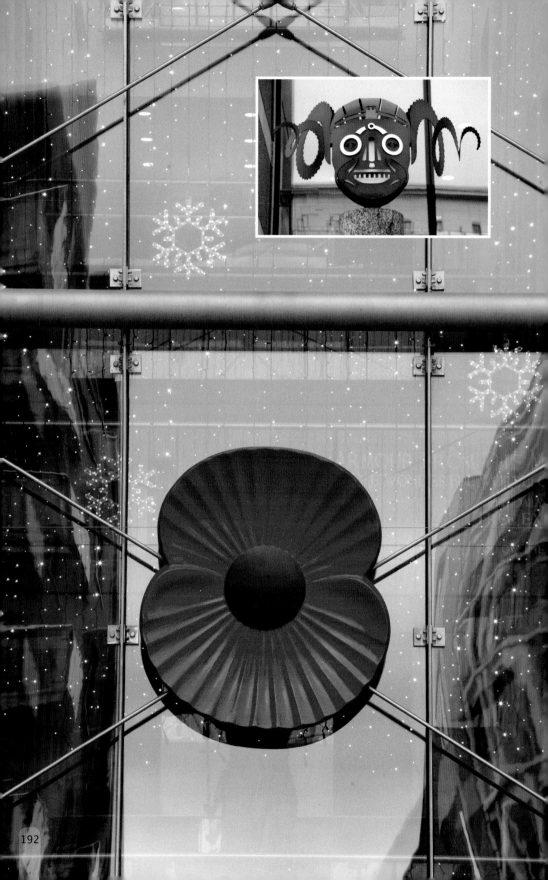

◀ *Next to Clarence Dock is the world famous Royal Armouries. This multi-million pound purpose-built structure houses a major part of the nation's collection of armour and weaponry from throughout the ages.*

▼ *Princess Exchange, which was designed by Carey Jones Architects in 1999. This superb building, with its sharp, bow-like front, leads us into the Whitehall Riverside, another exciting development in Leeds, which has turned previously run-down industrial land into something that Leeds can be proud of.*

▲▼*Whitehall Riverside.*

194

▲▶ *The highly reflective surfaces of modern structures create interesting patterns.*

◀▼ *The Calls Landing. Throughout the 19th century and early 20th century The Calls was the dockland of Leeds. The area contains many warehouses, which have since been converted into offices and luxury living spaces.*

▼ *Apartments on The Calls.*

▼ *Boats still travel the Aire & Calder Navigation, but now more for pleasure than commerce.*

▲ *A sculpture at Brewery Wharfe.*

▲ *Details of the sculpture at Brewery Wharfe.*

▼ *A metal heron looks out over the Aire & Calder Navigation at Brewery Wharfe.*

TEMPLE MILL

Perhaps one of the most unusual mills to be found in Leeds is the iconic Temple Mill. It was built in 1838 for the industrialist John Marshall, who had made his fortune from flax spinning. This building was seen as his crowning glory to a very successful business career. It was designed by Joseph Bonomi, who had used a number of Egyptian temples, most notably the Temple of Horus at Edfu, as his influence. The building was years ahead of its time and had a number of unusual features including a grassed roof which aimed to keep in the humidity needed for flax spinning. According to folklore, it is believed that sheep were kept on the roof to graze on the grass, and the story goes that one day one of them tumbled through a skylight, killing a worker below. At present the building remains empty, but there has been talk about renovating this beautiful and unique edifice.

▼▶ *Keeping with Leeds' tradition of the shopping arcade, DLG Architects created the Light. Originally it had been the headquarters of the Leeds Permanent Building Society, and it had been constructed in the early 1930s. During the 1990s the property was taken over by Leeds City Council and a 61–metre tower was demolished.*

As well as shops the Light includes a hotel, health club, nightclub, bars, a restaurant and the city's only central cinema.

▲Clad with large reflecting panels, the Leeds Shopping Plaza (formerly the Bond Street Shopping Centre) was built by John Brunton & Partners of Bradford, between 1974 and 1978.

▲ *The unmistakeably Gothic styled Church Institute building, built in 1866. In 1980 it was converted into shops.*

▼▶ *Once the premises of Leek & Westbourne Building Society, now the building is a Starbucks.*

▲ *Built in the Italianate style, the very grand Leeds Club was constructed in 1863 for the growing professional classes. Although Cuthbert Brodrick was a member of the club, it is not known whether he was responsible for the building's design.*

◀ *The Leeds Law Society Offices was originally built in 1795 as the home and consulting rooms for the surgeon William Hey.*

◀▼ *The Jolly Barrelman in Dortmund Square, on the Headrow. The statue is the work of the German artist Arthur Schulze-Engels.*
   It was a gift from the people of Dortmund to the people of Leeds when the two cities were twinned in 1990.

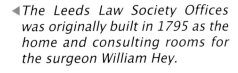

▲▶*Drydock – an interesting bar near the university.*

▼*Old Broadcasting House. Formerly belonging to the BBC, this building was later bought by Leeds University.*

LEEDS UNIVERSITY

As well as being one of the largest universities in the United Kingdom, Leeds University is also one of the fastest growing. Today it has over 33,000 full-time students, which is a major achievement as it only had 1,750 students in 1939. The university can trace its origins back to 1874, when it began as the Yorkshire College of Science. Lectures were first given in rented premises on Cookridge Street. In 1884 the college amalgamated with the medical school and three years later it joined with Manchester and Liverpool. It was an association that was to last until 1904, after which Leeds acquired an independent university status.

In 1877 the Yorkshire College commissioned the architect Alfred Waterhouse to design a purpose-built college. He had already designed Owens College, Manchester, and therefore he was considered the ideal candidate. It was hoped that £60,000 could be raised to complete the building, but the project was seriously in danger of floundering when their fundraising campaign only raised £20,000. Fortunately, the Clothworkers' Company of London came to their rescue and donated the balance. The company saw this as an ideal opportunity because they were keen to progress the scientific knowledge of the industry. It was due to this that the first building became the School of Textiles and Design (Woollen Division).

Three years later the chairman of the college council, Sir Edward Baines, donated £3,000. This resulted in the construction of the Baines Wing. In 1890 Waterhouse started work on the Great Hall. This magnificent building was constructed using red brick and was finished with bands of stone.

Perhaps the most distinctive and well-known of the university buildings is the Parkinson Building. This Portland-stone faced building with its soaring tower has become a Leeds landmark. Intended as a central arts and administration block, it was constructed with money donated by Frank Parkinson. The architects for this project were Lancaster, Lucas & Lodge. Just a short distance up the road the Mechanical Engineering Building, with its eye-catching fibreglass relief above the front entrance, can be found. It was designed by Allan Johnson and made by Alec Dearnby in 1961.

The campus of Leeds University is vast (as would be expected to accommodate the large number of students and faculties), but what is more it also covers an exciting range of architectural styles. It is certainly a treat for those interested in beautiful buildings.

▶ *The Parkinson Building.*

The Parkinson Building.

▲ *The Parkinson Building.*

▲◀*The fibreglass relief above the entrance to the Mechanical Engineering Building.*

▲ *The statue of Henry Rowland Marsden, Mayor of Leeds (1873–75) and philanthropist. He is considered to have been the most popular of the Victorian Mayors of Leeds. The statue was produced by local sculptor John Throp.*

▼ *Panels around the base show his involvement in education and industry.*

MONUMENT TO QUEEN VICTORIA

▲ *Queen Victoria's Monument standing in Woodhouse Moor Park.*

Originally this monument stood in front of the town hall on Victoria Square, but it was moved to Woodhouse Moor in 1937, when the square was remodelled. Following the death of Queen Victoria in 1901, it was decided to create a memorial in her memory. A committee was formed and a fundraising scheme was launched. Almost £8,000 was raised by subscription.

George J. Frampton was commissioned to design the memorial and surrounds but his plans for the square proved too costly; these included raising the level of the square, building a balustrade around it and surrounding the monument with trees. His scheme also included building broad carriage drives on either side of the statue and demolishing properties opposite the town hall to create a sweeping vista to the railway station.

▼ *The figure representing Peace.*

▲ The Royal Crest.

▲ A flowerbed in Woodhouse Moor Park.

Fortunately, the plans to demolish the properties were quickly abandoned when it was discovered how costly it would have been to purchase them. Plans for the 30ft bronze statue were approved and on 27 November 1905 the monument was unveiled by the Lord Mayor, Edwin Woodhouse. The monument consists of Queen Victoria sitting regally on top of a base made from Portland stone, and on either side there are bronze figures representing Peace and Industry. Sadly, Industry is no longer there.

Today, the monument stands among the flowerbeds and trees on Woodhouse Moor Park. It is, perhaps, a befitting place for Queen Victoria's monument to be sited because in 1858, while opening the town hall, she visited the park and was serenaded by 26,000 Sunday School children singing hymns.

Queen Victoria
on top of the
monument.

▲ *The Free Library near to the University.*

▶ *A detail above the windows of the Free Library.*

DUKE OF WELLINGTON

Another statue which also once stood in front of the town hall, and was moved to Woodhouse Moor in 1937, is Baron Carlo Marochetti's bronze figure of the Duke of Wellington. The statue was sculptured in 1855 and cost £1,500 to make. The commission had been somewhat controversial for Marochetti was Sardinian by birth, and many considered that the task of creating a statue of such a nationally important figure should not have gone to a foreigner.

▼ *The Duke of Wellington.*

This was formerly a grammar school, built in 1958 by E.M. Barry, and now it is the University Business School.

The glass extension to the University Business School was added in 1995 by Carey Jones Architects.

Leeds Innovation Centre, next to the University Business School.

KIRKSTALL ABBEY

The evocative ruins of Kirkstall Abbey have long been a favourite with both artists and photographers, and standing in this picturesque setting it is easy to see why. Construction started on the abbey in 1152 and amazingly took only 30 years to complete. It was to remain the home of a community of Cistercian monks until the Dissolution of the Monasteries under Henry VIII in 1539. The life of a monk at Kirkstall would have been hard and austere, with little time for idleness. When not performing their religious duties the monks would be working the land, in the workshops or even tending the flocks of sheep, for the abbey obtained much of its income through the sale of wool - a 15th-century document records that by 1301 the abbey owned 4,500 sheep and lambs.

▲ A row of columns and the Gothic vaulted ceiling in the nave.

Kirkstall Abbey in the dawn light.

After the Dissolution of the Monasteries the property was granted to Thomas Cranmer, the Archbishop of Canterbury, but it was restored to the Crown after he was burnt at the stake in 1556 for his beliefs. The years that followed were unkind to the abbey and much of the fabric of the buildings was plundered for other building projects around the city; some of the stone was used to construct the present Leeds Bridge. Today this venerable old ruin, which still retains the power to capture our imagination, is lovingly cared for by Leeds City Council and its future is in good hands.

◄ A plaque for the Leeds Waterfront Heritage Trail by the abbey.

▲ *A stone coffin at Kirkstall Abbey.*

ADEL CHURCH

For those interested in church architecture, a trip out of the city centre and into the suburbs is a must, for the church at Adel is a treat not to be missed. Widely considered to be one of the best remaining examples of Norman architecture in the country, St John the Baptist's Church is a Grade I listed, 12th-century building with many outstanding features. As such, its importance cannot be overestimated.

Perhaps one of its best known features is the elaborately carved stone doorway and the bronze Sanctuary Ring which was cast in York in 1200. There is an interesting story concerning the Sanctuary Ring. If a couple were too poor to buy a wedding ring they could be married in the church porch. Grasping the Sanctuary Ring, they would announce 'with this ring I thee wed'. Sadly, the original ring was stolen in 2002 and today it is a replica that adorns the door. Originally the church had a large stone porch; however, it was removed in 1816. Unfortunately, this has caused the stonework to deteriorate as it is open to the elements.

The word Adel comes from the Anglo-Saxon word *adela* meaning a muddy or boggy place. It is believed that there had been a church at this site prior to this Adel Church as there is an 11th-century charter which refers to the Church of St John of Adela. At one time the parish of Adel stretched over a considerable area but this has diminished over the years. The church is located near the site of the Roman fort of Burgodunum, which had been built on the ancient route from Ilkley to York. Two stone coffins that date from Norman times can be found at the gate of the church as well as some Roman and Saxon stones. In 1926 Adel was merged into the Borough of Leeds.

▲ *The fabulously carved entrance to the church.*

▲ The Sanctuary Ring on the door of St John's.

PARKS IN LEEDS

As well as the seven major parks in Leeds (which are, Golden Acre, Kirkstall Abbey Estate, Lotherton Hall Estate, Middleton Park, Otley Chevin Park, Roundhay Park and Temple Newsam Estate), there are also many community parks, playgrounds, areas of local green space and nature conservation areas.

Perhaps one of the most famous of Leeds' numerous parks is Roundhay. The name is derived from the Anglo-Saxon words *rund haeg* meaning a round enclosure. Originally, during the 13th century, the park was used by the De Lacy family for hunting. The entire estate was bought by Thomas Nicholson in 1803. He proceeded to develop the natural features of the surrounding land and made it into an impressive country estate, which included many delightful features such as a ravine, woodland walks, waterfalls and landscaped gardens. In 1811 work began on constructing a mansion, which took 15 years to complete. The building was designed by John Clarke and was built in the Greek Revival style.

▼*A path leading through Roundhay Park.*

▲ *A fountain on the upper lake in Roundhay Park.*

As with all fashionable parks, Roundhay has a folly in the form of a mediaeval gateway. This sham castle once possessed a wooden roof so that dinners and social events could take place within. The park also has a 33–acre lake called the Waterloo Lake. It took just two years to construct by a workforce made up of soldiers returning from the Napoleonic wars.

▲ The folly in the shape of a castle. It is not known who actually built it, but it is thought that it could have been constructed by George Nettleton in the early 19th century.

▲ A passage through one of the castle's towers leads to a path through the woods.

Looking across Waterloo Lake.

*Barran's Fountain. In 1882
Sir John Barran presented
the park with this grand
drinking fountain.*

242

The estate was acquired by the Mayor of Leeds, Sir John Barran, in 1871 for the people of the city. It was officially opened on 20 September 1872 and 100,000 attended the opening ceremony. In 1882 the park was presented with an ornate drinking fountain by Sir John Barran and it soon became known as Barran's Fountain.

◀▼ *Details of Barran's Fountain.*

▲▶ Oakwood Clock at Roundhay.

ELLAND ROAD

▲ *Elland Road Stadium is the home of Leeds United AFC.*

▼ *The statue of the late Billy Bremner stands outside the grounds of Leeds United AFC. Billy was captain of Leeds United from 1966 to 1976 and has since been voted the club's greatest player of all time.*

▲In the early 1990s the stadium received a multi-million pound redevelopment.

THE HEADINGLEY
CARNEGIE STADIUM

▲▼*Known as the Headingley Carnegie Stadium, the grounds were sponsored by Leeds Metropolitan University from 2006. The stadium is the home of Yorkshire County Cricket Club.*

▲▶ *It is also the home of the Rugby League team the Leeds Rhinos, and the Rugby Union team Leeds Carnegie (also known as the Leeds Tykes).*

▼ *The Carnegie Stand was built in 2006.*

HAREWOOD HOUSE

▲ *A tree in the grounds of Harewood.*

No book on Leeds would be complete without the inclusion of the stunning Harewood House, which is located seven miles out of the city centre on the road to Harrogate. The house was built in 1771 for the Lascelles family, who had purchased the estate after making their fortune producing sugar in the West Indies. The house was designed by John Carr and Robert Adam, while much of the furniture was by Thomas Chippendale, who had been born locally at Otley. The grounds were the work of Lancelot 'Capability' Brown, the famous English landscape gardener responsible for many of the gardens and parks belonging to the grand homes of England.

Harewood House is still the home of the Lascelles family and the seat of the Earls of Harewood. The present and 7th Earl is George Henry Hubert Lascelles, the eldest son of the 6th Earl and Mary, Princess Royal. He is first cousin to the Queen and 42nd in line to the throne.

▼ *In the grounds of the Harewood Estate, hidden among the trees, is the delightful 15th–century Church of All Saints.*

The estate is owned and managed by the Harewood House Trust and is open to the public throughout most of the year. It won a Large Visitor Attraction of the Year award in 2003 and remains one of West Yorkshire's most popular places to visit.